#movements

#IAmAWitness
Confronting Bullying

Jessica Rusick

Abdo & Daughters

An Imprint of Abdo Publishing
abdobooks.com

abdobooks.com

Published by Abdo Publishing, a division of ABDO, PO Box 398166, Minneapolis, Minnesota 55439. Copyright © 2020 by Abdo Consulting Group, Inc. International copyrights reserved in all countries. No part of this book may be reproduced in any form without written permission from the publisher. Abdo & Daughters™ is a trademark and logo of Abdo Publishing.

Printed in the United States of America, North Mankato, Minnesota
052019
092019

 THIS BOOK CONTAINS RECYCLED MATERIALS

Design: Aruna Rangarajan, Mighty Media, Inc.
Production: Mighty Media, Inc.
Editor: Liz Salzmann
Cover Photographs: AP Images (back background), Shutterstock (front background, front figure)
Interior Photographs: Design elements, Shutterstock; AP Images, pp. 8–9, 15, 16–17, 29 (top left); Flickr, p. 19; Gage Skidmore/Flickr, p. 22; iStockphoto, pp. 4–5, 12; Jeffrey Beall/Flickr, p. 11; Mighty Media, Inc., p. 21; Shutterstock, pp. 3, 7, 13, 25, 27, 28 (bottom), 29 (top right), 29 (bottom all)

Library of Congress Control Number: 2018966470

Publisher's Cataloging-in-Publication Data
Names: Rusick, Jessica, author.
Title: #IAmAWitness: confronting bullying / by Jessica Rusick
Other title: Confronting bullying
Description: Minneapolis, Minnesota : Abdo Publishing, 2020 | Series: #Movements | Includes online resources and index.
Identifiers: ISBN 9781532119309 (lib. bdg.) | ISBN 9781532173769 (ebook)
Subjects: LCSH: Bullying in popular culture--Juvenile literature. | Bullying in schools--Prevention--Juvenile literature. | Bullying--Law and legislation--Juvenile literature. | Protest movements--Juvenile literature.
Classification: DDC 305.23--dc23

CONTENTS

#IAmAWitness 4

Bullying History & Prevention 6

Bullying Laws 10

The Rise of Cyberbullying 14

Bystanders to Bullying 18

Witness Emoji 20

Witness the Results 24

Beating Bullying 26

Timeline 28

Glossary 30

Online Resources 31

Index 32

In October 2015, a new emoji became available for mobile device keyboards. It looked like a talking eye. At the same time, the hashtag #IAmAWitness started appearing in social media posts. The emoji and hashtag were both part of an anti-bullying campaign started by the Ad Council.

Smartphones and social media sites have allowed bullying to spread beyond school buildings and the school day. Mean messages can reach someone at any time. And they can go viral, possibly reaching millions of people. This is called cyberbullying.

Many laws and organizations have taken a stand against bullying and cyberbullying. Most of these campaigns have focused on those who bully or those who are bullied. But I Am A Witness was different. It spoke directly to bystanders.

Bystanders are the silent majority who witness bullying. They may feel

LET'S TALK TERMS

Bullying is repeated, aggressive, and unwanted behavior directed toward a person. Someone who bullies has a real or perceived power over the person they bully. Cyberbullying is bullying that happens through digital platforms.

A NOTE ON LABELS

Experts say it is important to label the behavior and not the person. Instead of "bully," say, "someone who bullied." Instead of "victim," say, "someone who was bullied."

About one in every three students reports being bullied at school.

nervous to speak out against bullying for fear of being bullied themselves. But I Am A Witness made speaking out easier. The eye emoji let witnesses call out bullying with the touch of a finger. And they could use the #IAmAWitness hashtag to post anti-bullying messages. Together, these digital tools empowered bystanders to take a stand against bullying.

Cyberbullying is a product of modern technology. But bullying is not just a modern occurrence. It is likely that humans inherited bullying from our earliest ancestors. At one time, bullying was a social strategy for maintaining power in a competitive society. Individuals who bullied may have been more likely to survive and reproduce.

Early bullying was largely physical. As human culture changed, so did bullying. Language allowed nonphysical bullying to develop. For example, humans were able to hurt others by spreading rumors.

Though bullying has long been a part of human society, it was not widely studied until the 1970s. Dr. Dan Olweus, a Norwegian psychologist, was among the first to study bullying. His research followed schoolboys in Stockholm, Sweden. Olweus observed their traits and behaviors to find differences between those who bullied and those who were bullied.

Olweus's research helped change common beliefs about bullying. In the 1970s, many considered bullying a natural and acceptable part of growing up. But Olweus's research showed that bullying in schools was a social problem that made students feel unsafe. Olweus believed this problem could and should be prevented.

In the 1980s, Olweus became the first to develop a bullying prevention program for schools. The goal of the Olweus Bullying Prevention Program

Dan Olweus is considered the pioneer
of bullying research. He believed
feeling safe at school was a human right,
and that bullying violated this safety.

A fourth-grade class in Scandia, Minnesota, listens to their teacher discuss bullying. The school used the Olweus Bullying Prevention Program.

was to reduce bullying and foster a caring school culture. The program trained students, teachers, and parents to recognize bullying. And those involved in bullying were provided guidance through counseling.

In 1993, Olweus developed a definition of bullying that is still widely used today. Olweus's definition had three parts. The first was that bullying was an intentional behavior. Second, it was repetitive, happening more than once and involving the same people. Third, it featured a power imbalance. Those who bullied had higher status than those who were bullied. For example, higher status could mean being physically stronger or being more popular.

In the 1990s, Olweus began working with American educators to bring his program to the US. Today, hundreds of US schools have adopted it. But it was not until 1999 that bullying became a major topic of discussion

Bullying Laws

In 1999, a national tragedy brought bullying into the US spotlight. On April 20, students Eric Harris and Dylan Klebold carried shotguns and other weapons into Columbine High School in Littleton, Colorado. Their shooting spree killed 13 people and injured 20. At the time, it was the deadliest high school shooting in the nation's history.

Afterward, people tried to understand what caused the tragedy. One popular theory was that Harris and Klebold had been bullied and wanted revenge. Later, this theory was shown to be untrue. But at the time, it sparked a national conversation about bullying. There was a push to pass state laws addressing bullying in schools.

In 1999, Georgia became the first state to pass an anti-bullying law. Today, all 50 states have one. Each law is different. But many require schools to investigate incidents of bullying. This means schools must train staff members to recognize bullying and help those involved. It also means developing ways for students to report bullying.

Many laws recognize several types of bullying behavior. Physical bullying means hurting someone's body or damaging their possessions. Verbal bullying is saying or writing cruel things, including threats. And social bullying means hurting someone's social standing. This includes spreading rumors or leaving someone out of a group on purpose.

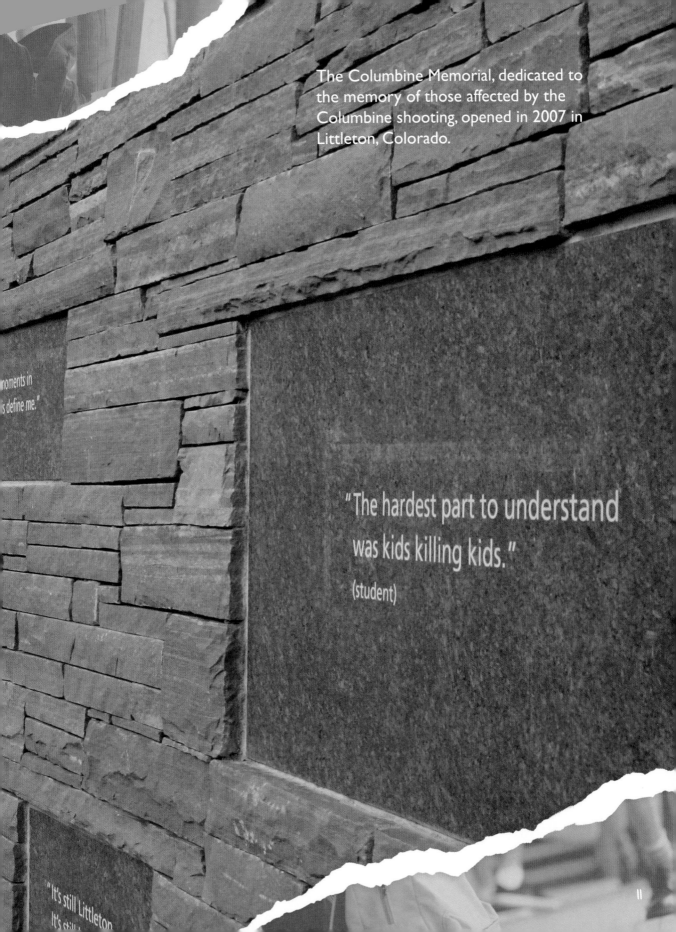

The Columbine Memorial, dedicated to the memory of those affected by the Columbine shooting, opened in 2007 in Littleton, Colorado.

noments in
s define me."

"The hardest part to understand was kids killing kids."
(student)

"It's still Littleton
It's still

Bullying is often seen as something that happens to children and teens at school. However, bullying happens to adults in social situations and in the workplace too.

Research has not proven whether laws have helped reduce bullying. Health experts agree laws could strengthen anti-bullying efforts in schools. However, schools face challenges in implementing the laws.

One challenge is limits imposed by the specific state's law. Some states only allow schools to intervene in bullying that takes place on school property. But this doesn't help address cyberbullying. Schools also have to consider students' civil rights, such as privacy and free speech. This can limit how far schools can go to stop bullying.

Another threat to the effectiveness of anti-bullying laws is new technology. The first anti-bullying laws addressed face-to-face bullying. But in the mid-2000s, social media sites such as Facebook and Twitter became popular. Social media was a powerful tool for connection. But it could also be abused. Over the next years, cyberbullying became a growing concern.

WHY ARE PEOPLE BULLIED?

Anyone can be bullied. But people perceived as physically or socially different are at a greater risk. People can be bullied for their weight, economic status, race, gender identity, and more. Bullying can have negative consequences. Someone who is bullied may face mental health issues such as depression and anxiety.

WHY DO PEOPLE BULLY?

Some people who bully others think it will increase their popularity. Others bully to cope with trauma, such as family-related issues. Bullying may temporarily let someone forget about their problems. But it is not a positive solution. Those who bully are more likely to drop out of school and face aggression problems in the future.

The Rise of Cyberbullying

The term *cyberbullying* was first used around 2000. Cyberbullying is digital or online bullying. It can take place within text messages, apps, and on social media sites. Today, 95 percent of US teens spend time online. Data from the Cyberbullying Research Center shows that 16 percent of teens have been cyberbullied at some point in their lives.

By the mid-2000s, cyberbullying was on the rise. In 2006, a study from the journal *Pediatrics* found that in five years, cyberbullying had increased by 50 percent among teens and preteens. In the following years, several widely reported suicides brought cyberbullying to national attention in the US.

Two of these suicides were 13-year-old Megan Meier and 18-year-old Tyler Clementi. Both Meier and Clementi had been cyberbullied before their deaths. Some media outlets speculated that cyberbullying played a role in their deaths.

Experts find that suicidal behavior is caused by a complex web of factors. Bullying is just one factor that can affect someone's mental health. So, bullying alone may not lead to suicide. However, many people felt Meier's and Clementi's deaths highlighted the unique concerns of cyberbullying.

Cyberbullying can be more harmful than face-to-face bullying. Those who bully online can use anonymous or fake identities. This anonymity can

Meier's mother, Tina Meier, holds photos of her daughter. Megan Meier was bullied through the social network MySpace.

After Tyler Clementi's death, New Jersey senator Barbara Buono helped pass an Anti-Bullying Bill of Rights.

embolden those who bully to be extra cruel. They cannot see the reaction of the person being bullied. So, they may not realize the harm they are causing.

Cyberbullying can also happen any time of day or night. In-school bullying ends with the school day. But someone can send a mean message at any time.

Because cyberbullying doesn't happen in a physical place, it can be hard for adults to spot. And, studies show teens may not want to report cyberbullying. One reason for this is they fear their parents won't allow them to go online anymore if they do.

Because cyberbullying presents unique issues, many states updated their anti-bullying laws between 2006 and 2010. The updated laws addressed cyberbullying in addition to in-person bullying. Outside the government, organizations formed with the sole purpose of addressing cyberbullying.

In 2007, Megan Meier's mother, Tina Meier, founded a cyberbullying prevention organization. The Megan Meier Foundation provides resources and information to help those who have faced cyberbullying. Similarly, in 2011, the Tyler Clementi Foundation was started to fight cyberbullying and improve safety in schools. The organizations are two of many that fight cyberbullying worldwide.

Bystanders to Bullying

Whether bullying takes place online or in person, discussions of the issue commonly focus on those who bully and those who are bullied. But there is another group to consider. Bystanders are those who witness bullying. They may encourage bullying to continue. They may defend someone being bullied. Or they may be silent witnesses, neither approving of nor stopping the bullying.

Although bystanders may not be directly involved, bullying can still have negative effects on them. Witnesses are more likely to experience depression and anxiety than those who do not witness bullying. But when bystanders speak out against bullying, the results can be positive. When a bystander intervenes, bullying is more likely to stop.

On social media, millions of people can witness one instance of cyberbullying. Research shows that 88 percent of teens on social media have witnessed online bullying. But few have stood up for someone being bullied. Many teens say they want to help. But they either don't know what to say or fear being bullied themselves.

The Ad Council wanted to help silent bystanders speak up.

TAGGED

"When bystanders intervene, #bullying stops w/in 10 seconds. #IAmAWitness"
—Bully Movie
(@bullymovie, Twitter)

Past Ad Council PSAs addressed smoking, wildfire prevention, drug use, and drunk driving.

The Ad Council is a nonprofit organization that makes public service announcements (PSAs). Since 1942, these PSAs have raised awareness about social issues and inspired change. And in 2015, cyberbullying came into the spotlight.

Witness Emoji

The Ad Council wanted to empower teens to make a positive difference when they witnessed bullying. The council's directors knew teens often used emojis in digital messaging. So, they decided to make an emoji to call out cyberbullying. It would be the first-ever emoji designed for a social cause.

Teens could use the emoji whenever and wherever they saw cyberbullying. The emoji would send a message that someone witnessed the bullying and didn't approve of it. The emoji was part of a larger campaign called "I Am A Witness."

The Ad Council asked ad agency Goodby Silverstein & Partners to design the emoji. Angie Elko and Patrick Knowlton worked on the design. From the beginning, Elko and Knowlton knew they wanted to use an eye. They liked the play on words between *I* in "I am a witness" and *eye* in "eyewitness."

THE POWER OF EYE CONTACT

The Witness emoji's design was inspired by science. Psychologists have found that images of eyes affect human behavior. When people see an eye, they are more likely to behave well. This is because the eye creates a feeling that someone is watching.

The Ad Council's I Am A Witness campaign included posters and flyers featuring the eye emoji.

YouTube star Grace Helbig was involved in an #IAmAWitness video campaign. The video won a Shorty Social Good Award.

But an eye alone was not active enough. The emoji needed something else. Elko and Knowlton brainstormed hundreds of ideas. Eventually, they found what they were looking for. Their Witness emoji was an eye within a speech bubble. The eye symbolized a watchful gaze. And the speech bubble symbolized speaking up.

On October 22, 2015, I Am A Witness launched. Apple and Google helped bring the Witness emoji to 240 million smartphones worldwide. It became part of Apple emoji keyboards. Teens could also download a separate I Am A Witness keyboard. The keyboard featured anti-bullying stickers, GIFs, and more emojis! The stickers had messages such as "see bullying," "want to talk?" and "you are awesome." Teens now had a toolbox to use when they saw cyberbullying.

Social media sites helped promote the Witness emoji. Snapchat designed custom filters. Reddit changed its alien mascot, Snoo, to have the emoji as its eye. And whenever people used the hashtag #IAmAWitness on Twitter, the Witness emoji appeared!

The Ad Council also turned to YouTube to help promote the emoji. YouTube stars, including Lizzie Velasquez and Ricky Dillon, appeared in a national advertisement to raise awareness. In the commercial, they read mean comments posted by viewers of their own YouTube videos. The stars then encouraged everyone to stand up to online cruelty by using the Witness emoji.

YouTube stars also posted videos on their own channels. Each video directed teens to the campaign's website, iwitnessbullying.org. Here, teens could find more anti-bullying resources. Under a "Send Kindness" section, users could post positive images and videos. People could then send these messages to anyone who needed them!

TAGGED

"I am so honored to be a part of the @AdCouncil's #IAmAWitness anti-bullying campaign."
— Lizzie Velasquez
(@littlelizziev, Twitter)

The I Am A Witness campaign empowered teens to take a stand against bullying. Six months after its launch, there were 60,000 conversations on social media about the campaign. On Twitter and Instagram, 37,000 people posted using the hashtag #IAmAWitness. And the custom keyboard was used more than 270,000 times!

The campaign helped make a difference in how teens perceive bullying. The Ad Council talked to teens before and after its campaign launched. Before the launch, 46 percent of teens said they knew what to do when they saw bullying. After six months, this number increased to 56 percent. Fifty-six percent of teens also said they felt their actions could make a difference against bullying. This was up from 43 percent!

The campaign was praised for its unique approach to bullying prevention. But some anti-bullying advocates wondered if the emoji was enough. Professor Jennifer Grygiel argued that social media sites needed to do more to stop cyberbullying. She suggested sites could review any post that was flagged with the Witness emoji.

TAGGED

"Sometimes emojis speak louder than words. 👁 #WorldEmojiDay #IAmAWitness"
—Adobe Project 1324
@project1324, Twitter

24

THE FACES OF #IAMAWITNESS

Patrick Knowlton is the Creative Director at Goodby Silverstein & Partners. He has held this position since 2011. As Creative Director, Knowlton helps design ad campaigns for large companies and products. He helped design the Witness emoji and the I Am A Witness campaign.

Angie Elko is a designer and art director working in San Francisco, California. In 2015, she was a Senior Designer at Goodby Silverstein & Partners. In this role, she helped design the Witness emoji and the I Am A Witness campaign.

Lizzie Velásquez is a YouTube star and anti-bullying advocate. Velásquez has a medical condition that prevents her from gaining weight. This led people to cyberbully her about her appearance. Today, Velásquez travels around the US to speak out against bullying. In 2015, she partnered with the I Am A Witness campaign to promote bystander intervention.

"The most important opinion anyone can ever have about you is your own!! Show the world how incredible you are no matter what anyone says!!"
— Lizzie Velásquez
(@littlelizziev, Twitter)

Lizzie Velásquez

Beating Bullying

In 2018, other anti-bullying campaigns took the place of I Am A Witness. In May, First Lady Melania Trump launched the Be Best campaign. Its goal was to help children live happy, healthy lives. Be Best encouraged kids to fight cyberbullying by using social media in positive ways. The campaign also promoted values such as kindness and respect.

IF YOU ARE BEING **BULLIED**

- Tell the bully to stop in a clear voice.
- Laugh off the comments or walk away.
- Do not fight back.
- Tell an adult about the bullying.

IF YOU ARE BEING **CYBERBULLIED**

- Don't respond to cyberbullying messages.
- Take screenshots so you can report the bullying.
- Block the person who is sending mean messages.

IF YOU ARE A **BYSTANDER**

- Be kind to those who are bullied.
- Use tools like the Witness emoji to stand up to online bullying.
- Join causes such as the Million Upstander Movement.

In September, the Ad Council launched Because of You. It encouraged teens to reflect on their words and actions. In doing so, the campaign hoped to create a more positive and inclusive culture.

In November, the Tyler Clementi Foundation announced its Million Upstander Movement. The movement's goal is to turn bystanders into "upstanders" who speak out against bullying. The foundation

Melania Trump's Be Best campaign has its roots in her own experience with being bullied.

hopes to recruit one million people by fall 2020. To join the movement, upstanders sign an online pledge to respect, support, and encourage others.

The I Am A Witness campaign was a unique approach to bullying prevention. It has impacted the lives of teens everywhere. And the Witness emoji lives on in millions of Apple keyboards worldwide. Bystanders can still use it to say #IAmAWitness!

TIMELINE

Dr. Dan Olweus, a Norwegian psychologist, becomes one of the first people to study bullying in schools.

The term *cyberbullying* starts being used.

1970s

2000s

1980s

1999

Olweus develops one of the first bullying prevention programs for schools.

The Columbine shooting in Littleton, Colorado, sparks a national conversation about school bullying in the US.

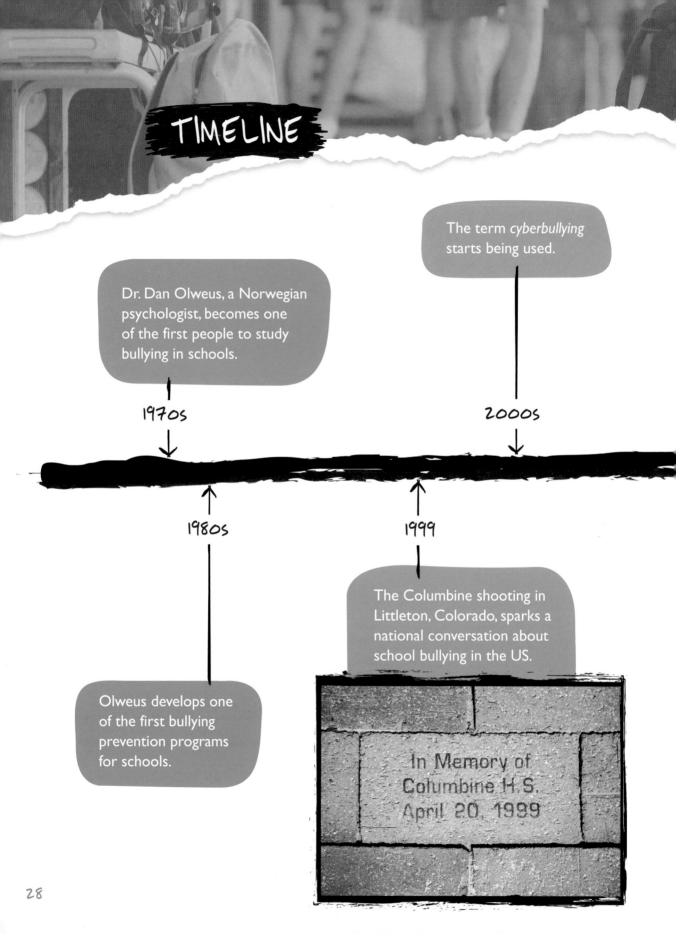

In Memory of
Columbine H.S.
April 20, 1999

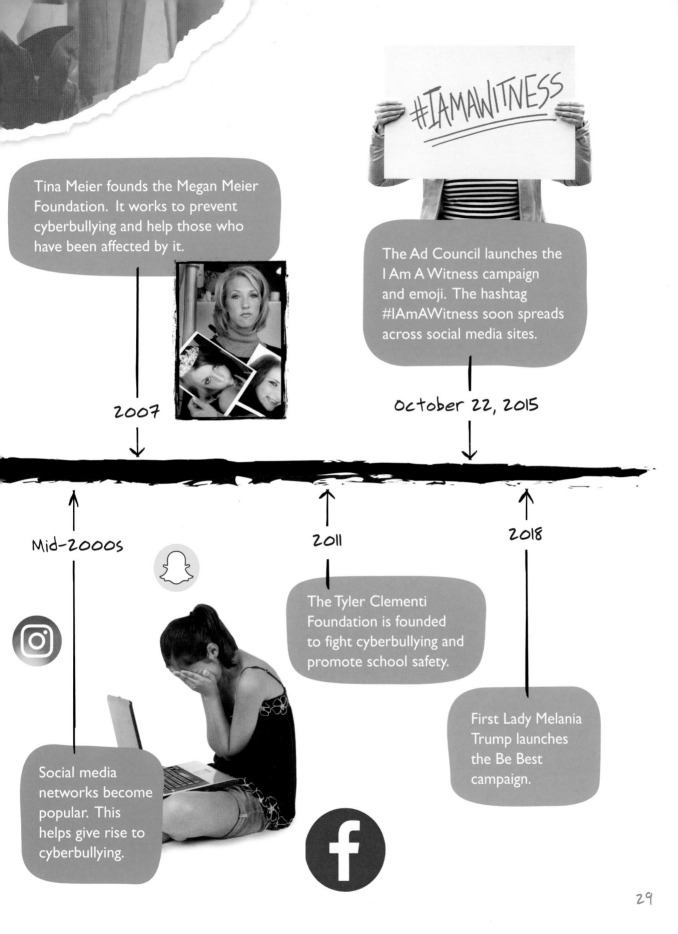

Tina Meier founds the Megan Meier Foundation. It works to prevent cyberbullying and help those who have been affected by it.

The Ad Council launches the I Am A Witness campaign and emoji. The hashtag #IAmAWitness soon spreads across social media sites.

2007

October 22, 2015

Mid-2000s

2011

2018

The Tyler Clementi Foundation is founded to fight cyberbullying and promote school safety.

First Lady Melania Trump launches the Be Best campaign.

Social media networks become popular. This helps give rise to cyberbullying.

GLOSSARY

advocate—a person who defends or supports a cause.

anonymous—not named or identified. The state of being anonymous is anonymity.

brainstorm—to come up with a solution by having all members of a group share ideas.

bystander—a person standing near but taking no part in what is happening.

definition—a description or explanation of something.

embolden—to make someone feel braver or bolder.

emoji—a small symbol or picture that can be typed in an email, a text, or an online post.

empower—to help people gain control over their own lives.

gender—the behaviors, characteristics, and qualities most often associated with either the male or female sex.

hashtag—a word or phrase used in social media posts, such as tweets, that starts with the symbol # and that briefly indicates what the post is about.

imbalance—when two things or conditions are not equal.

intervene—to interfere in order to affect, change, or prevent. An instance when someone intervenes is an intervention.

social media—websites or smartphone apps that provide information and entertainment and allow people to communicate with each other. Facebook and Twitter are examples of social media.

status—a social or professional standing, position, or rank.

suicide—the act of killing oneself. Someone who wants to kill him- or herself is suicidal.

technology—scientific tools or methods for doing tasks or solving problems.

trauma—extreme physical injury or emotional upset.

viral—quickly or widely spread, usually by electronic communication.

ONLINE RESOURCES

Booklinks
NONFICTION NETWORK
FREE! ONLINE NONFICTION RESOURCES

To learn more about #IAmAWitness, please visit **abdobooklinks.com** or scan this QR code. These links are routinely monitored and updated to provide the most current information available.

INDEX

Ad Council, 4, 18–19, 20, 23, 24, 26
anti-bullying laws, 4, 10, 13, 17
Apple, 23, 27

Be Best, 26
Because of You, 26
bullying
    origins, 6
    recognition, 9, 10
    reporting, 10, 17, 24

California, 25
civil rights, 13
Clementi, Tyler, 14
Colorado, 10
Columbine High School, 10
cyberbullying, 4–5, 6, 13, 14, 17, 18–19, 20, 23, 24, 25, 26–27
Cyberbullying Research Center, 14

Dillon, Ricky, 23

Elko, Angie, 20, 22, 25

Georgia, 10
Goodby Silverstein & Partners, 20, 25
Google, 23
Grygiel, Jennifer, 24

Harris, Eric, 10

I Am A Witness, 4–5, 20, 23, 24, 25, 26, 27
iwitnessbullying.org, 23

Klebold, Dylan, 10
Knowlton, Patrick, 20, 22, 25

Megan Meier Foundation, 17
Meier, Megan, 14, 17
Meier, Tina, 17
mental health, 13, 14

Million Upstander Movement, 26–27

Norway, 6

Olweus, Dan, 6, 9
Olweus Bullying Prevention Program, 6, 9

Pediatrics, 14

research, 6, 9, 13, 14, 18

school shootings, 10
social media, 4–5, 13, 14, 18, 23, 24, 26
Stockholm, Sweden, 6

Trump, Melania, 26
Tyler Clementi Foundation, 17, 26–27

Velasquez, Lizzie, 23, 25